The Superbook of
TRICKS AND PUZZLES

George Beal

KINGFISHER BOOKS

Contents

This edition published in 1986 by Kingfisher Books Limited
Elsley Court, 20–22 Great Titchfield Street, London W1P 7AD
A Grisewood & Dempsey Company
© Grisewood & Dempsey 1986

BRITISH LIBRARY CATALOGUING IN PUBLICATION DATA
Beal, George
  Tricks and puzzles.
   1. Puzzles—Juvenile literature
   2. Tricks—Juvenile literature
  I. Title
  793.73   GV1493

ISBN 0–86272–200–4

Designed by the Pinpoint Design Company
Typeset by Southern Positives and Negatives (SPAN), Lingfield, Surrey
Printed in Hong Kong

—Tricks and Puzzles—

This book contains nearly a hundred tricks, puzzles and games to amuse and entertain you and your friends. There are riddles to decipher, and practical problems to solve. You will find optical illusions, games to play, and tricks with which to surprise other people.

All you will need are a few things you can find at home – paper and pencils, string, scissors, corks, and other common household items. In the centre of the book, between pages 18 and 23, there are cards and shapes which you will need in order to perform certain tricks. Carefully remove and cut these out – and then, together with some skill and imagination, you have everything you need!

Of course, if you get stuck, all the answers are at the back of the book. But with a little thought, all the puzzles in the book can be solved. And with a little practice, you will find you can perform tricks and surprise your friends.

Have fun!

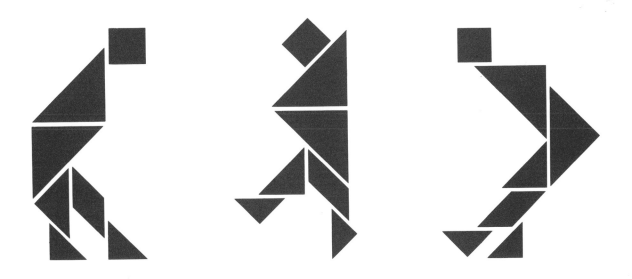

Thought

1. Magic Cards

To do this trick, you will need seven special cards, each with 64 numbers on them. It is also an advantage if you are good at adding numbers together in your head! If you turn to the centre pages, you will find the cards, ready to cut out. The cards should be handed to a friend, who is then asked to think of a number between 1 and 127, but not to reveal it. To make this more interesting you could ask the friend to choose his or her age. He or she is then asked to return to you every card on which the number appears. You will then be able to tell your friend the number he or she thought of.

You can do this, because the cards have been numbered in a special way. Let us suppose your friend thought of the number 63. The number 63 appears on cards A, B, C, D, E and F. Now look at the *first* number, which appears at the top left hand corner on each of the cards handed back to you. The numbers are 1, 2, 4, 8, 16 and 32. Add these numbers together, and you get 63. If the number 7 was chosen, then that number will be found only on cards A, B and C. The first numbers on each of those cards are 1, 2 and 4, which added together, make 7.

This seems to be some sort of trick, but in fact, it is simply a matter of how the numbers on the cards are arranged. Here is another example to try. You have been handed the cards A, B, C, D and G. The first numbers at the top left hand corner are 1, 2, 4, 8 and 64. Added together, they make 79, which is the number which would have been chosen if those cards had been selected.

2. Finding Someone's Age

Ask someone to write down the number of the month in which they were born. Now, tell them to multiply it by 2. Next, tell them to add 5 and multiply the answer by 50. Next, add their present age to the total, and then subtract 365. You then ask the number left. Add 115, and you will now be able to tell the person's age. Looking at the total, the figures on the right will be the age, and those on the left will be the number of the month of birth. Here is an example:

Suppose your friend is 12 years old, and was born in July. He or she writes down:

The number of the month	**7**
Multiplied by 2	**14**
Add 5	**19**
Multiplied by 50	**950**
Add present age (12)	**962**
Subtract 365	**597**

Your friend tells you the total, which is 597. To this, you add 115, making 712. The figures at the right are 12 – your friend's age – and the figure at the left is 7, which is his or her birthday month; in this case, July.

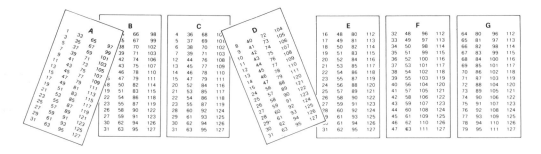

Reading

3. Finding a Number

This is quite an old trick, but it still works and surprises people: Think of a number; double it; add 12. Add five; subtract three; divide the total by two. Take away the number first thought of. You can now tell the number remaining. Here is an example:

Think of a number	**82**
Double it	**164**
Add twelve	**176**
Add five	**181**
Subtract three	**178**
Divide by two	**89**
Subtract number first thought of	**−82**
Answer is	**=7**

In fact, the answer is *always* 7!

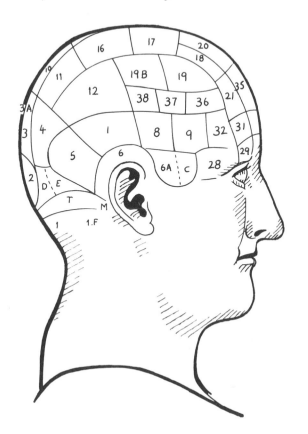

4. The Word in the Book

Ask your friend to take a book, open it at random and choose any word in the *first ten lines* and *within ten words of the end of the line*. Now tell him or her to double the number of the page and multiply the answer by 5, and then add 20. Now, ask your friend to add the number of the line, and then another 5. The total must be multiplied by 10. Now add the number of the word in the line. Finally, ask your friend to subtract 250 from the total, and tell you what's left. The last figure will tell you the number of the word on the line; the last figure but one will be the number of the line, and the figures remaining will tell you the page number. Here is an example:

Your friend opens a book at random, and the page happens to be **152**.

He picks the fifth word on the fifth line, 'same'.

Double the number of the page	**304**
Multiply by 5	**1520**
Add 20	**1540**
Add number of line (5)	**1545**
Add 5	**1550**
Multiply by 10	**15500**
Add number of word in line (5)	**15505**
Subtract 250	**15255**

So the word will be found in the book on page 152, line 5, word 5.

5: Nine Cards in a Square

First you will need nine cards, each 4 cm square. Every card should be numbered as shown, with the numbers reading across in plain figures, and those reading downwards in small circles. What you have to do, is to arrange the nine cards in a square, the numbers in circles forming upright lines, and the plain numbers horizontal lines. They must be arranged so that the three figures in each line, whether upright or horizontal, make 13 when added together.

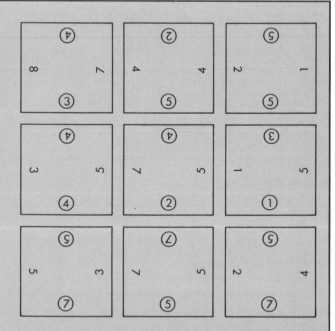

6: Rectangles

Can you say how many rectangles there are in this diagram?

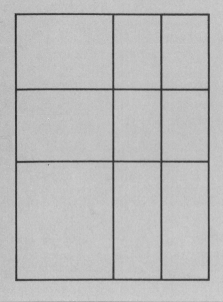

7: The Hexagon

How many triangles can you find in this hexagon?

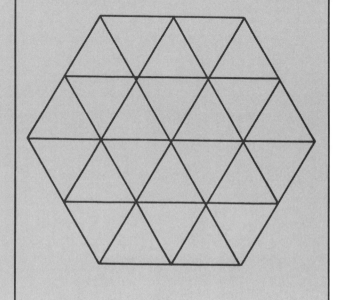

It Out

8. The Bookworm

Three books of a three-volume set are standing on a shelf as shown in the picture. A bookworm tunnels its way through from the first page of the first volume to the last page of the last volume. The cardboard on each part of the cover of each book is 2 mm thick, and the pages in each book occupy a total thickness of 302 mm. How far did the bookworm travel?

9. The Number 37

If you multiply the number 37 by the following numbers, it will give these results:

$$37 \times 3 = \mathbf{111}$$
$$37 \times 6 = \mathbf{222}$$
$$37 \times 9 = \mathbf{333}$$
$$37 \times 12 = \mathbf{444}$$
$$37 \times 15 = \mathbf{555}$$
$$37 \times 18 = \mathbf{666}$$
$$37 \times 21 = \mathbf{777}$$
$$37 \times 24 = \mathbf{888}$$
$$37 \times 27 = \mathbf{999}$$

10: The Same Six Figures

The number 142,857, when multiplied by any number up to and including six, will always give an answer containing all six of the original figures, like this:

$$142,857 \times 1 = \mathbf{142,857}$$
$$142,857 \times 2 = \mathbf{285,714}$$
$$142,857 \times 3 = \mathbf{428,571}$$
$$142,857 \times 4 = \mathbf{571,428}$$
$$142,857 \times 5 = \mathbf{714,285}$$
$$142,857 \times 6 = \mathbf{857,142}$$

11. Dividing It Up

A man once divided £9 between two fathers and two sons, each father and each son receiving £3. How did he do it?

12. Fun With a Calculator

If you have a pocket calculator, you can play a number of little tricks with it. For instance, set the following figures on the display: 710.77345 Now turn the calculator upside-down and you can see: SHELL 'OIL. Of course, the 'letters' are not exactly right, but they are clear enough to read the message. Try these others, by setting up the figures on the display, and then turning the calculator upside-down: 993.7108 (BOIL EGG); 55373045 (SHOELESS); 378809 (GOBBLE). You can make up your own 'message' if you use the following figures to represent letters: 1 = I; 2 = Z; 3 = E; 4 = H; 5 = S; 6 = g; 7 = L; 8 = B; 9 = G; 0 = O. Remember, however, when setting up a word, that the figures should be entered in *reverse* order.

13. Strange Symbols

Here is a sequence of what appear to be very odd symbols. They are, in fact, in a proper logical sequence. Can you draw in the symbol which should follow?

14. The Difference

What is the difference between twice twenty-five and twice five and twenty?

15. Dozens

What is the difference between six dozen dozen and half a dozen dozen?

16. Herrings

Five herrings are divided among five people. Each person has a herring, and yet one remains on the dish. How can this be?

17. Making Six Into Three

Change the following six upright strokes to make three, without rubbing out or taking any away.

I I I I I I

18: A Strange Sum

How can you take one from nineteen and leave twenty?

19. Cutting the Cloth

A shopkeeper had to divide a piece of cloth into metre lengths. She found that she could cut off one metre per second. The piece of cloth was 60 metres in length. How long did she take to cut up all the lengths?

20. Strange Addition

1. Add five to one, and make it four
2. What can be added to nine to make it six?

21. The Mouse

A mouse found a box in which there were a number of ears of corn. It started to bring them out, three ears on each journey. It took nine journeys to remove them all. How many ears were there in the box?

22. More Strange Symbols

Above there are some odd symbols. Here are some others. Can you understand what this says?

23. The Eight Matches

Here are eight matches. Can you make $2\frac{1}{2}$ dozen out of them?

24. Circle of Coins

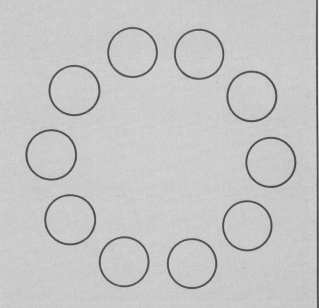

Arrange ten one-penny coins (or counters) in a circle, as shown, *'heads' upwards*. Now starting from any coin you like, number them out loud, 1, 2, 3 and so on. When you reach the fourth coin, turn it over, to show 'tails'. Then, again, starting from any coin you like, count 1, 2, 3 and 4, and again turn over the fourth coin. Try to carry on like this until all the coins have been turned over to show tails. You can count either backwards or forwards. Coins showing tails must be counted in as you move round, but the count of four must fall upon a coin showing heads.

25. The Square and Triangles

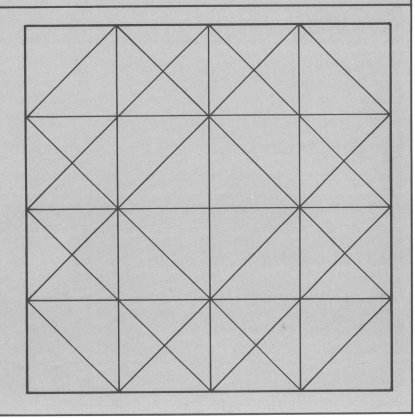

Look closely at this square. It contains a number of squares and a number of triangles. Can you say how many there are of each?

Logical

26. Family Party

A family gathering included 1 grandfather, 1 grandmother, 2 fathers, 2 mothers, 4 children, 3 grandchildren, 1 brother, 2 sisters, 2 sons, 2 daughters, 1 father-in-law, 1 mother-in-law and 1 daughter-in-law. Yet there were only seven people present. How can this be?

27. The Portrait

A picture of a person hangs in the living room, and a visitor asks the owner: 'Who is portrayed in that picture?' The owner replies:

'Uncles and brothers have I none,
But that man's father is my father's son.'

Who is shown in the portrait?

28. Hard-Boiled Eggs

How many hard-boiled eggs can a hungry person eat on an empty stomach?

30. Forwarding the Mail

Arthur Williams had to go to Brussels for a conference. He left Jenny Jones in charge. 'While I'm away,' said Arthur 'I would like you to forward all my mail to my hotel in Brussels.' 'Certainly,' said Jenny. However, after Arthur had been gone for three hours, Jenny realized that all mail for the office came into a special mailbox, which was kept locked. Mr Williams had forgotten to give her the key. She telephoned the airport, but the plane had left, so she was unable to post any letters on. Some days later Arthur phoned his office in London, and asked why no mail had been sent on to him. Jenny explained why, and Arthur agreed to post the mailbox key to her. He duly did this, but still no mail was forwarded on to him in Brussels. When he did arrive back at his office, he sent for Jenny and fired her on the spot. Was this fair?

29. The Houses and the Pipes

The plan shows three houses marked A, B and C. All are in an enclosed private square. At the entrance to the square are the mains supplies for gas, electricity and water. Each of the houses needs only one of these services. House A needs only water, house B needs only gas, and house C needs only electricity. The pipes must be laid in such a way as to bring the three services to the houses requiring them. The pipes must not cross each other, nor must they pass outside the square.

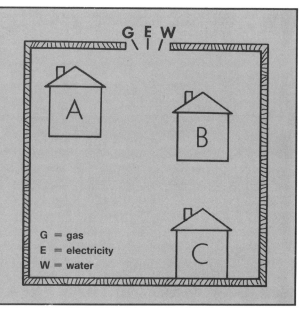

G = gas
E = electricity
W = water

Thought

31. The Orchard

A farmer had an orchard in which there grew twelve apple-trees, as shown in the diagram. When he died, his will stated that the orchard should be divided between his four children. Each child was to have a piece of orchard containing three apple trees, and each piece of land had to be of the same shape. How was the division made?

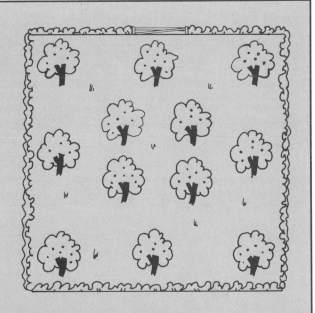

32. Balancing a Stewpot

At a summer camp, the cook was given a large stewpot, a paving stone, four wooden poles and four pieces of flat iron. He lit the fire in the centre of the stone, and fitted the four poles into recesses on each corner of it. But the uprights were too far from the centre to support the pot. The wooden uprights could not be moved further in, since they would burn. The four pieces of iron were not quite long enough to reach from one pole to the next, and they were certainly not long enough to be placed across the fire diagonally. How did the cook make the support for his stewpot?

33. The Farmhouse

Another farmer had five children and he made a will stating his wish that the farmhouse should be divided equally between them, and the land also. As shown in the diagram, the land surrounding the house had ten fruit trees, and he wished each child to have two of them. Each child was to have a same-sized and same-shaped piece of land, on each of which there were two fruit trees. How was the land divided?

34. The Two Belgians

Two Belgians arrived in London, and went to lunch at the Savoy Grill. One Belgian was the father of the other Belgian's son. How could this be?

35. The Pigs in the Sties

Joe once bought ten pigs in the market, but when he got home, he realized that he had only nine small sties to keep them in. He was puzzling over this, when his neighbour, Tom, walked over. Joe explained his difficulty. 'Nothing to it, Joe,' said Tom. 'Just do as I say.' So, following Tom's instructions, Joe put the first two pigs in sty No. 1. Then he put the third pig into sty No. 2, the fourth in sty No. 3, the fifth in sty No. 4, the sixth in sty No. 5, the seventh in sty No. 6, the eighth in sty No. 7, and the ninth in sty No. 8. He then told Joe to take one of the pigs from sty No. 1 and put it in sty No. 9. 'Now you've got all the pigs in,' said Tom. Joe agreed, and was about to close up the sties, when he heard a grunting sound. 'Wait a minute, Tom.' he said. 'I've still got one pig left over!' What went wrong?

36. The Phone-In

Recently there was a television phone-in in which a well-known legal man was answering listeners' queries. He answered various questions, and then one man came on the line and said he wanted to know about the matrimonial laws. 'Yes,' said the legal man. 'What is it you wish to know?' 'I would like to know if the law allows a man to marry his widow's sister,' said the listener. 'The law has nothing to say in the matter,' said the legal man. 'But if you are the man in question, I very much doubt if you'll ever get the opportunity!' Why should this be?

37. The Home Secretary

In the British House of Commons, the Home Secretary rose to report on crime statistics. 'There has been an alarming increase in the number of deaths from poisoning,' he said. 'probably because so many poisons are easy to come by. This means that the number of undetected murders rose from a total of 1400 in the previous year to 2600 last year.'

'Absolute nonsense,' retorted the Leader of the Opposition. Why should the statement be described as nonsense?

38. The Ship's Ladder

A ship was at anchor in a harbour with a rope ladder hanging from the edge of the deck down into the water. Six rungs at the bottom of the ladder were now under water; each rung was 3 cm wide, and the rungs were 25 cm apart. The tide was rising at the rate of 40 cm per hour.

How many rungs would be under water at the end of two hours?

39. Balancing the Books

Mr Tompkins came home from the office one day, and found his wife looking rather puzzled. 'What's the matter?' he asked. 'It's about the bills I paid today,' said Mrs Tompkins. 'I took £10 and paid the butcher £4. That left me £6. Then I paid the grocer £2.50, which left me £3.50. I bought some things from the chemist which cost £2, leaving me £1.50, and then I paid the paper bill which was £1.50. That left me nothing.' 'What's wrong with that?' asked her husband. 'I always keep a note of things,' she said, 'so I made two columns of what I spent, and what I had left, like this:

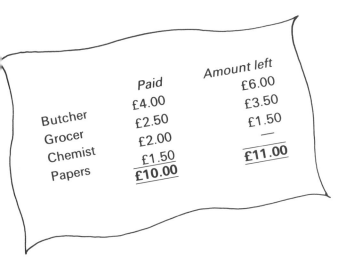

	Paid	Amount left
Butcher	£4.00	£6.00
Grocer	£2.50	£3.50
Chemist	£2.00	£1.50
Papers	£1.50	—
	£10.00	£11.00

What I can't understand is, where has the other pound gone to? I think I must have lost it!'

40: The Dream

A doctor and a detective were having a discussion about their cases. The detective told him the story of a man who was watching television with his wife. They were watching a 'cops and robbers' type of film, with car-chases and shooting, and all the usual sort of mayhem. The man, however, fell asleep, and in his dream he was actually taking part in the story he had been watching on television. He was being chased in his car by some villains, and was speeding along, when he came to a railway crossing. Although the lights were red, he decided to take a risk, and crashed across the line. Only then did he see an express train roaring down upon him. Meanwhile, in the living-room, the television film ended, and the man's wife switched off the set, and noticing that her husband was asleep, shook him by the shoulder. It was just at that moment in his dream that the express train was about to hit him. The shock was so great that the man collapsed and died.

'That's absolute nonsense,' said the doctor. Why did he say that?

41: At the Bank

A messenger arrived at an office one day with a parcel. At the enquiry desk, the messenger asked for Miss Robinson. 'I have to hand this parcel over to Miss Robinson personally,' explained the messenger. 'Well,' said the girl at the enquiry desk. 'As a matter of fact, I'm Miss Robinson.' The messenger was about to hand over the parcel, but hesitated. 'Er – I'm sorry, but how do I know you *are* Miss Robinson? The girl smiled. 'I think I can prove that,' she said, and felt in her handbag. She produced a photograph of herself, and showed the messenger. 'There. A pretty good likeness, isn't it?' she asked. 'Oh yes, said the messenger, quite satisfied. 'Here's your parcel.' What mistake had he made?

42: The Roman Coin

This coin (of which both sides are shown) was taken to a London auction house by a woman who said she had found it while digging in her garden. She knew that her house had been built on the site of an old Roman encampment, since she had found one or two small items in the past. But this was a fine coin, and in remarkable condition. She would like it put into the firm's next sale. The experts examined the coin, and one turned to the woman and said 'I'm afraid we can't accept this. In fact, you are lucky we haven't sent for the police and had you arrested.' Why did the expert say this?

43: The Two Indians

One day, in a Red Indian encampment in the United States, a big Indian, Strong East Wind, and a little Indian, Happy Hunter, took their tomahawks and set off for the distant hills. Happy Hunter was the son of Strong East Wind. But Strong East Wind was not the father of Happy Hunter.

How can this be the case?

44: The Factory

The managing director of a factory was very concerned about the loss of tools, equipment and other things through pilfering by employees, and decided to employ a new security officer who would be responsible for detecting any more thefts. The new security person was duly taken on. 'Most of my employees are honest,' said the managing director, 'but it isn't fair if a few dishonest people are getting away with it.' 'Don't worry,' said the security officer, 'I'll give this matter all my attention.'

After a month or two, things started to improve, but the security officer was not satisfied, and in particular, was suspicious of a certain man called Joe Foxwell. In the course of his job, Joe regularly took a wheelbarrow of all kinds of junk out of the factory, and down to the local dump. Each time he left the factory, Hawkins made a thorough search of Foxwell's barrow and person, but found nothing, except old rusty bits of metal, broken parts and other rubbish.

The months turned to years, and Foxwell regularly pushed his barrow out of the factory gates and down the road. At last, it came the time for Foxwell's retirement, and so he left the factory for ever. Many years later, the security officer was in a pub and ran into Foxwell. Naturally, they started to chat about the old days.

'I always suspected you, Joe, and I still think you were pinching something.'

'I'll tell you the truth,' said Joe. 'I was.'

'I knew it!' cried Hawkins. 'What were you stealing?'

Can you guess what Joe Foxwell was stealing?

Tricks and Games

45. The Clasped Hands

Tell someone you are able to clasp his or her hands together in such a way that he or she cannot leave the room without unclasping them. How?

46. Problem With Hands

Tell someone you can put something into his or her left hand which he or she cannot possibly take with his or her right. What is it?

47. Fives

At first glance, this looks like a card trick, but it is really just a way of arranging certain cards. You take all four of the 'fives' from an ordinary pack of cards. Now, arrange them in such a way (face upwards) that only four pips on each card are visible.

48. Aces and Courts

This is another puzzle using playing-cards. Take all the aces and picture cards from the pack, and discard the rest. What you have to do is to arrange the cards in four rows in such a way that neither across nor down are there two cards of the same value or suit in the same row. In other words you can only have (for instance) one King in any row downwards or across, and only one card from each suit. Each row must have a King, a Queen, a Jack and an Ace, and all four suits must be present.

49. Paper Shapes

Get some stiff paper, and cut out four shapes exactly like that shown below. Make the pieces as accurate as you can. Now the problem is to piece the four shapes together so that they fit accurately, and make the same sort of shape as that above, but much larger.

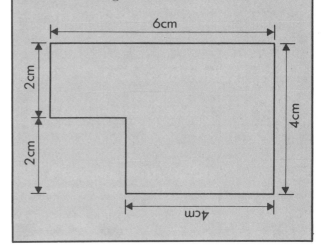

50. Floating Corks

For this, you will need seven ordinary corks from wine bottles. They should not be the tapering kind, but cylindrical. Now take a basin of water, and try to place the corks in the water so that they float *upright*.

51. Man of Many Parts

Turn to the centre pages, and you will find four cards each with a picture of a man on it. Cut them out carefully, and then try to piece them together so that instead of four rather strange figures, you have one single correct picture.

52. Squares and Discs

This is a game or puzzle which requires a number of squares and discs made so that they can be linked together. You can make these yourself, like those shown on the right. They should be made from some fairly stiff card. Each square card should be 6 cm square, and each disc should be 6 cm across. A slot 2 mm wide and 15 mm deep is cut in the exact centre of each side of the squares. It is best to trace the pattern from the designs illustrated here. The circular cards have three slots, each 2 mm wide and 15 mm deep. They are not equally spaced around the circumference, and the exact places for cutting should be traced from the pattern illustrated. You will need 48 of the square cards, and 10 of the discs. If you wish, you can make extra sets of these. The cards are made to slot together, and can then be used to build all sorts of models. Examples of some are shown here.

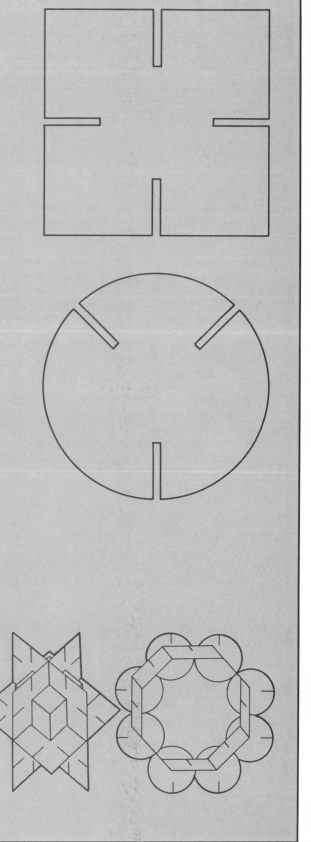

53. Cork and Bottle

For this, you need a clean wine bottle and a cork which is slightly too small for the bottle. It should, however, but just large enough to stay in the neck if placed there and not pushed. Try to blow the cork into the bottle. You will almost certainly fail. Yet the trick can be done. How?

54. Knotting the Ring

For this, you will need a short piece of thin cord or string, and a plain finger ring. One person holds the cord, and the other the ring. They are then asked to tie the cord in a knot around the ring, but each using one hand only.

55. The Treasure Map

If you turn to the centre pages, you will see four squares which are four pieces of a map of a treasure island. The island was once the haunt of pirates, and eight different pirate chiefs ruled from separate lairs. Then Captain Kidd arrived, and decided to stop the constant warring between the chiefs. So he made a number of roads, eight crossing the island in one direction, eight more at right angles to them, and others crossing diagonally. The roads were so arranged that the occupants of each lair had a clear road in each direction through the island without passing any other lair. The pirates have now gone, and their lairs are in ruins, but the map remains. It had been folded into four, but had been used so often that it had became tattered and torn into four pieces. After the island became independent, the Governor offered a reward to anyone who could place the four square pieces back together in their original positions. That means that there could be no two lairs on any road, either horizontal, vertical or diagonal.

Cut out the four squares carefully, and see if you can arrange them in the correct way.

56. Balancing a Pencil

Take an ordinary pencil and a penknife, and sharpen the pencil to the best point you can. Try to balance the pencil in an upright position on the tip of your forefinger.

57. Cutting a Postcard

Take an ordinary postcard, and cut it, keeping it in one piece, so that an ordinary person can step through it.

58. Lifting the Coin

Take five drinking straws, and cut each to a length of about 10 cm. Now take a five pence piece, and using *one straw only*, lift all the rest of the straws, plus the coin.

59. Two Dogs

The illustration shows two dogs, who are either asleep or dead. By adding just four more lines, can you bring the dogs back to life again?

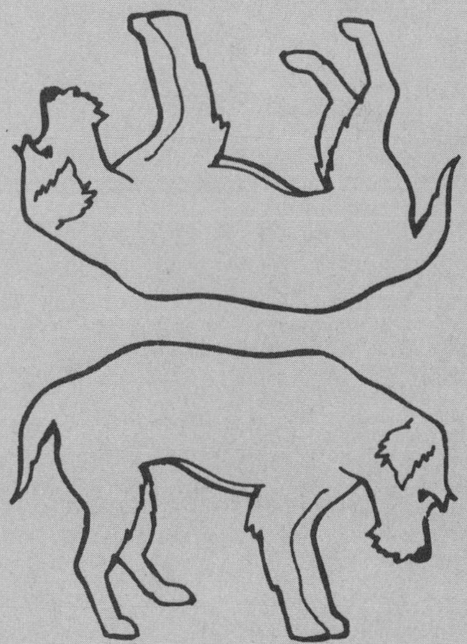

60. Unspillable Water

This is a trick which should be done in the kitchen! Take an ordinary wineglass, fill it with water, and place it so that the glass cannot be lifted without spilling all of the water.

61. Holding a Coin

A handkerchief is spread on flat upon a table, and a five pence coin placed at the centre. Now, can you pick up the handkerchief, move it so that it is held vertically, and still keep the five pence in position?

62. Looping the Scissors

Take a piece of strong string and place the two ends together so that the string is doubled. Pass the loop end through one of the bows of a pair of scissors, pass the opposite ends through the loop, and then through the second bow. Finally tie the ends of the string around a stick, as shown in the diagram. The puzzle is to free the scissors without untying the string, or slipping the string off the stick.

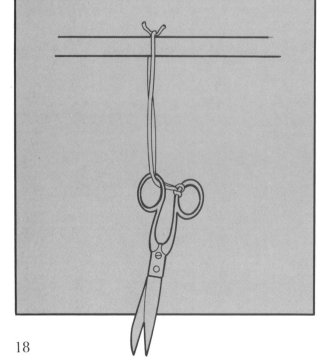

63. The Hole in the Paper

Take a piece of stiff paper, and cut a circular hole in the centre the size of a 5p coin. Ask anyone to pass a 10p coin through the hole without touching the coin or tearing the paper. It will seem impossible: the diameter of a 5p coin is less than that of a 10p. Yet it can be done. How?

64. Burglars and Detectives

From an ordinary pack of cards take the four Queens, Kings, Jacks and Aces. Discard the rest of the pack. Place the four Aces face upwards in a square on the table. You start a story based on the cards: 'In a large city, there were four houses, which were built in a square like this. In each of the houses, there lived a lady.' You now place a Queen on each of the Aces. 'One day, while all the ladies were sleeping, a burglar broke into each of the houses.' You place a Jack on each of the Queens. 'When the ladies discovered their houses had been burgled, they sent for the police, and four detectives arrived to investigate.' Now place the four Kings on each of the Jacks. Pick up each pack of four cards, and place them together to form one pack. Turn the pack over, and ask someone to cut it. 'The police investigation was successful' you say. Now start to deal the cards out face upwards in a square again, following the same order. You will find that one of the four packs will contain all the Aces, another all the Queen, another all the Kings, and another all the Jacks. When you have finished, you can point to each pack in turn and say 'Now, all the houses are safe again; all the ladies have got together for a party, all the burglars are in prison, and all the detectives are back at the police station.' The order in which each of these packs falls will vary according to where the pack was cut, so you must adjust your story to fit the order.

A			
1	33	65	97
3	35	67	99
5	37	69	101
7	39	71	103
9	41	73	105
11	43	75	107
13	45	77	109
15	47	79	111
17	49	81	113
19	51	83	115
21	53	85	117
23	55	87	119
25	57	89	121
27	59	91	123
29	61	93	125
31	63	95	127

B			
2	34	66	98
3	35	67	99
6	38	70	102
7	39	71	103
10	42	74	106
11	43	75	107
14	46	78	110
15	47	79	111
18	50	82	114
19	51	83	115
22	54	86	118
23	55	87	119
26	58	90	122
27	59	91	123
30	62	94	126
31	63	95	127

C			
4	36	68	100
5	37	69	101
6	38	70	102
7	39	71	103
12	44	76	108
13	45	77	109
14	46	78	110
15	47	79	111
20	52	84	116
21	53	85	117
22	54	86	118
23	55	87	119
28	60	92	124
29	61	93	125
30	62	94	126
31	63	95	127

D			
8	40	72	104
9	41	73	105
10	42	74	106
11	43	75	107
12	44	76	108
13	45	77	109
14	46	78	110
15	47	79	111
24	56	88	120
25	57	89	121
26	58	90	122
27	59	91	123
28	60	92	124
29	61	93	125
30	62	94	126
31	63	95	127

E			
16	48	80	112
17	49	81	113
18	50	82	114
19	51	83	115
20	52	84	116
21	53	85	117
22	54	86	118
23	55	87	119
24	56	88	120
25	57	89	121
26	58	90	122
27	59	91	123
28	60	92	124
29	61	93	125
30	61	94	126
31	62	95	127

F			
32	48	96	112
33	49	97	113
34	50	98	114
35	51	99	115
36	52	100	116
37	53	101	117
38	54	102	118
39	55	103	119
40	56	104	120
41	57	105	121
42	58	106	122
43	59	107	123
44	60	108	124
45	61	109	125
46	62	110	126
47	63	111	127

G			
64	80	96	112
65	81	97	113
66	82	98	114
67	83	99	115
68	84	100	116
69	85	101	117
70	86	102	118
71	87	103	119
72	88	104	120
73	89	105	121
74	90	106	122
75	91	107	123
76	92	108	124
77	93	109	125
78	94	110	126
79	95	111	127

1

51

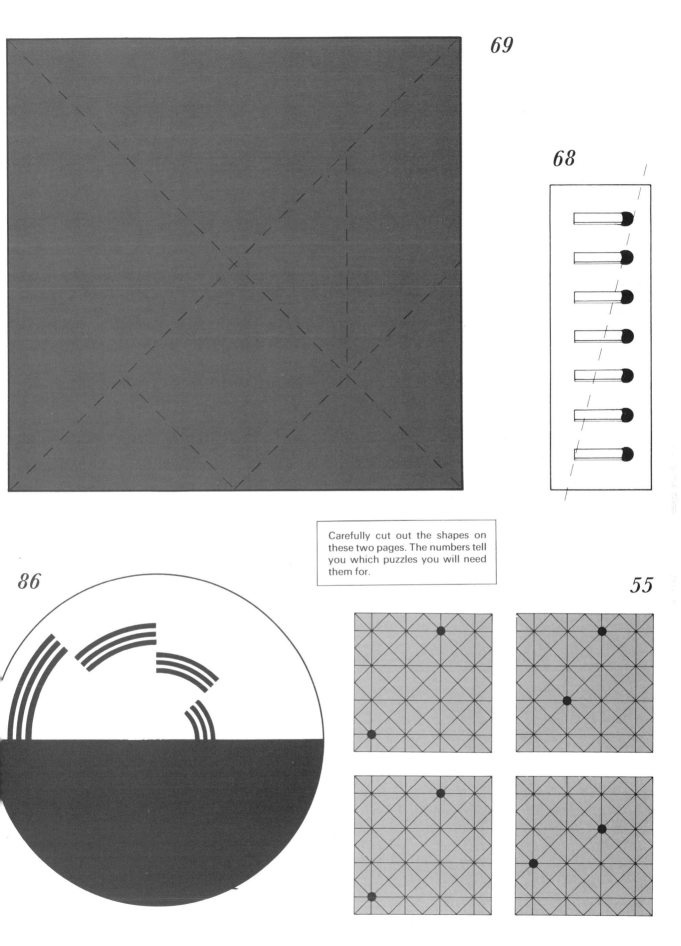

69

68

Carefully cut out the shapes on these two pages. The numbers tell you which puzzles you will need them for.

86

55

65. Camera Lucida

This is a simple way to help you draw small objects. First, place the small object you wish to draw on a book or books. Place a sheet of white paper on the table between yourself and the object, and on the far edge of the paper, rest the edge of a pane of glass. The glass should be about 25 cm square. Incline the glass towards you, and by gently moving the glass up and down you will eventually see in it the reflection of the object you wish to draw. Naturally, you will also see the paper through the glass.

To keep the glass in this position, rest it on a small book alongside. Take a pencil (a short one is best), and hold it on the paper under the glass, and see if you can see the reflection and the pencil point plainly at the same time. If either the pencil or the reflection looks 'double' while you fix your eyes on the other, it means that the object is either too near or too far away.

Move the book on which it rests backwards and forwards until you can see both reflection and the pencil point plainly. If you keep your eye perfectly still, you can now follow the reflection outline with the pencil, and so make a tracing of it upon the paper. The picture will be of the same size as the object, so only quite small objects can be drawn.

66. Paper Bands

Make three strips of paper, about 3 cm wide and 15 cm long, and make them into bands by pasting the ends together. Make the first band into a simple ring, as shown at 'A' in the diagram; the second should be given a twist before it is pasted, as at 'B' in the diagram; and the third should be given two twists, as shown at 'C' in the diagram.

Now cut each band along its length, as indicated by the dotted line in the diagram. You will now have two separate rings from the first (as at 'D' in the diagram), a single ring of half the width and twice the diameter from the second (as at 'E' in the diagram), and two rings linked together from the third (as at 'F' in the diagram).

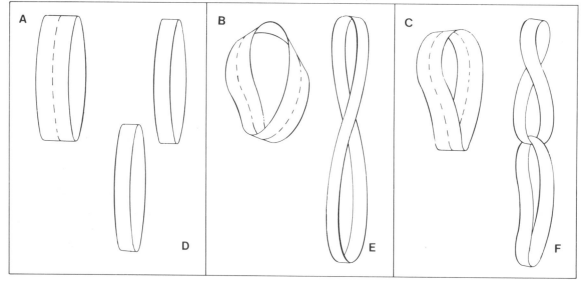

67. Voice Sounds

Find a spool, like those used for cotton thread, and stretch two rubber bands over the hole at one end, so that the two edges each half cover the hole. The two bands should be very close together, but not touching. Secure the bands on the side of the spool by binding wire around it, or else place drawing pins at the end of each band. Now place the other end of the spool to your mouth and blow. The sound coming out will be very like the human voice, which will vary according to the force of breath going through.

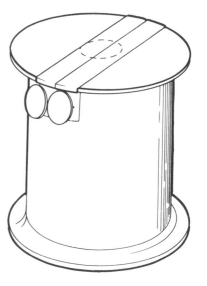

68. How Many Matches?

Here is a picture of a row of matches. It is also reproduced on the centre pages. Cut it out carefully, and then cut the whole drawing into two along the diagonal line. Place the two pieces together, as shown, and count the number of matches which will be seven. Now slide the upper part one stage along until the matches coincide. Count the matches again, and this time there will be only six.

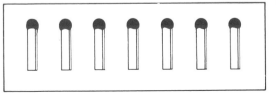
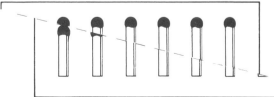

69. Tangrams

This is an old puzzle. You need the seven pieces of card which you will find, ready to cut out, on the centre pages. First of all, fit all the pieces together, and you will be able to make a square, as shown here. Now take all the pieces apart, and you can put them together to make all sorts of shapes and figures. A few examples are shown below.

Visual

70. Top Hat

The picture shows an old-fashioned top hat. Which is longer, the width of the brim or the height of the hat?

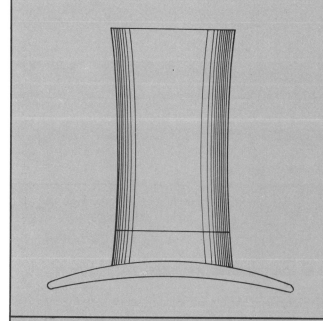

72. The Lampshade

Which is the shorter, the top of the lampshade, or the top of the stand below?

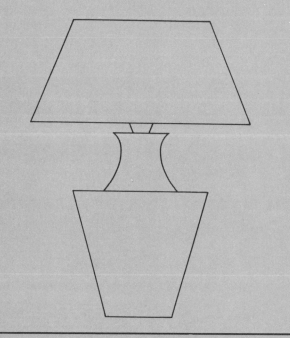

71. The Three Squares

Which of these 'squares' are really squares?

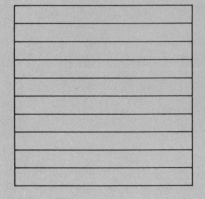 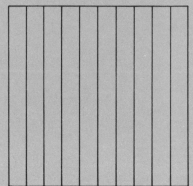

Illusions

73. The Three Men

We are so used to seeing drawings in perspective that we sometimes forget that the actual figures must vary in size to complete the illusion. The three men shown in the diagrams are all of exactly the same size, but because lines of perspective have been added, the nearest figure seems smaller than the farthest.

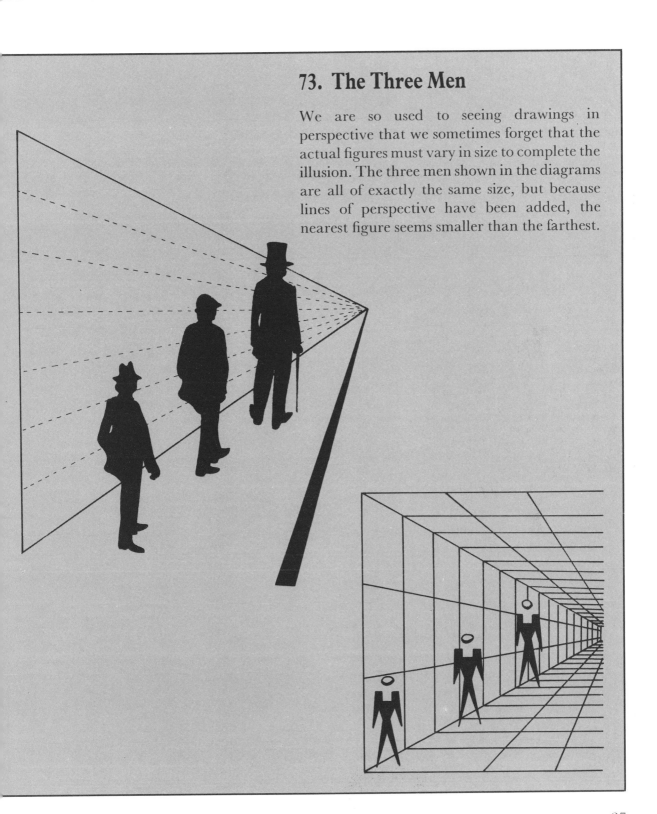

74. The Circles

(a) The circles in the centre of each of the two designs are equal in size.

(b) The inner circle of figure *1* and the outer circle of figure *2* are of the same size, while the inner circle of figure *2* and the inner circle of figure *3* are of the same size.

(c) The circle in the inner part of the angle appears to be larger than the circle at the outer end, but both are of the same size.

(d) The circle in the centre of the diagram is a true circle, but the lines surrounding it make appear to be out of true.

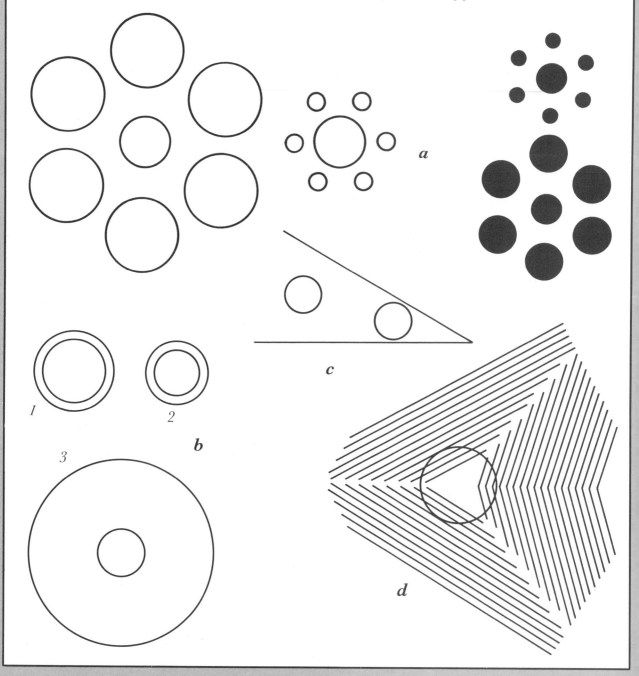

a

1

2

3

b

c

d

75. Black or White?

The arrow-shaped designs in the square can be seen either as black patterns on a white background, or white patterns on a black background.

77. The Booklet

Does this booklet open away from you, or does it open towards you?

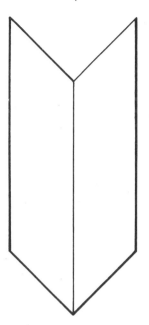

76. The Cubes

Does this diagram show cubes with white tops seen from above, or does it show them seen from below?

78. Rings in the Tube

Are you looking in the end of a tube with rings which opens towards the right or to the left?

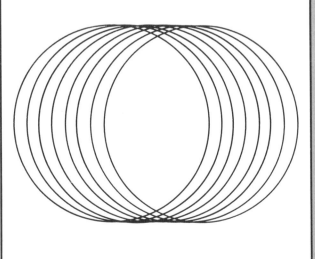

79. The Staircase

Are you looking down upon this staircase, or are you standing below looking up?

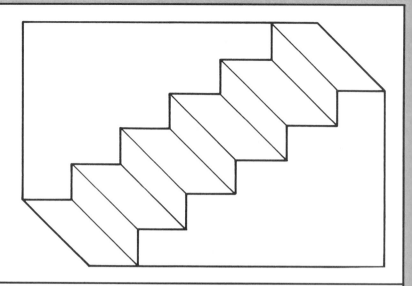

80. Parallel Or Not?

Here are five examples of lines which are actually parallel, but which appear to be converging. In A, it is because the parallels are crossed by short cross-lines. In B, the two parallel lines appear to be closer together at the centre, and in C, seem to be wider at the centre. In D and E, the lines again appear to be curved or bent. In each case, if the page is turned and held level with the eye, the illusion disappears.

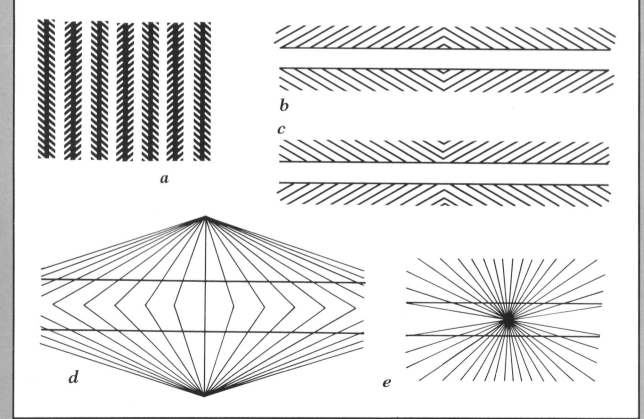

81. Which Line Continues?

Here is an illusion about which line meets which. In *(a)* would the short sloping line (if continued) meet the other sloping line? In *(b)* which of the two sloping lines on the left continues the sloping line on the right? Which is it in *(c)*?

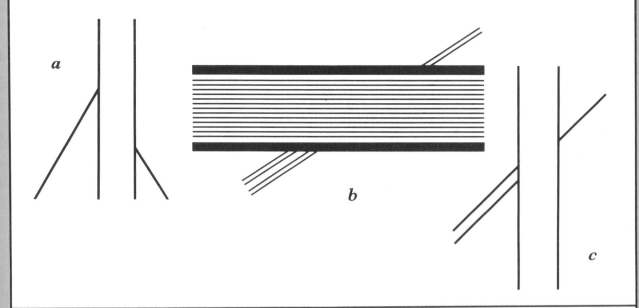

a

b

c

82. The Rotating Spiral

If this diagram of a spiral is held and rotated, it appears to grow larger or smaller, according to which way it is turned.

83. The Revolving Wheels

Here is a similar diagram. If you hold the page in front of you and twist the design with your wrists, the wheels appear to be turning.

84. Length Of the Lines

Here are three horizontal lines each with shorter lines added at each end. 'A' is a line divided into two by arrow-like angles. The distance *(i)* is exactly the same as the distance *(ii)*. In 'B', the two lines are both of exactly the same length.

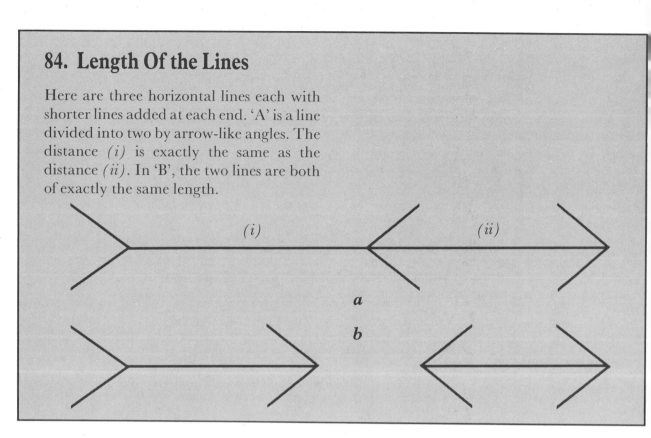

85. Black and White Squares

If you look at diagram 'A', your eyes will soon see dark spots at the points between the corners of the squares. If you move your eyes from one set of squares to another, you will find that the 'black spots' also appear to move.

Now look at diagram 'B.' This shows a block of white squares, and if you stare at this for a time, your eyes appear to see small white spots at the points between the corners of the squares.

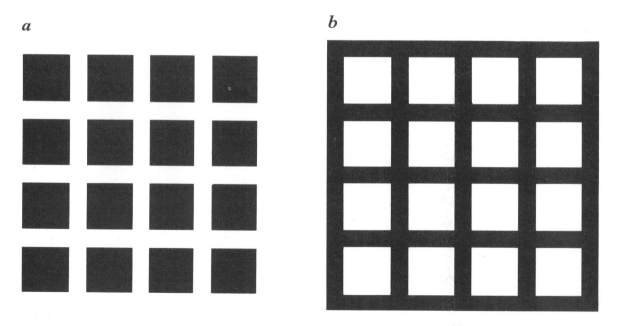

86. The Colour Disc

Turn to the centre pages, and cut out the disc shown. Pierce the point at the centre with a pin and thread a loop of string through the hole so the disc can be spun. If you spin the disc, a series of colours will be seen. When you spin the disc one way, the colours will appear to be red at the outside, and blue-green at the centre. In the other direction the colours will be in reverse.

87. The Table

Here is a picture of a skeleton-like table. The question is, are you looking at it from the top, or are you underneath, looking up? You will find that the positions will appear to change as you blink your eyes.

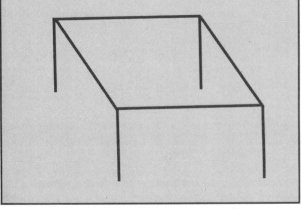

88. The Silhouette

Look steadily at the figure in silhouette shown here. Count up to 25, and then quickly move your eyes to a blank sheet of paper. You will see the shape – but now in white on the page.

89. The Dog In the Kennel

Here is a picture of a kennel and a dog. Hold the picture on a level with your eyes, and about 4 cm in front of your nose. Keep looking steadily, and you will see the dog move slowly into the kennel.

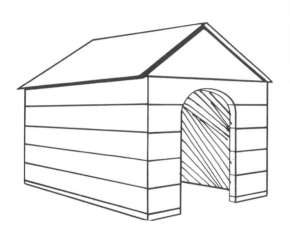

90. Vase or Profiles?

If you look at this picture, sometimes it will appear as a white vase on a black background, and sometimes as two profiles in black with a white background.

92. Where Is the Middle Rod?

Look at the three rods shown above. But are there three of them – and where does it join the base?

91. The Triangle

Here is a rather strange-looking triangle. Are you looking up at it from below, or are you seeing it from the side?

93. Odd Shapes Or Word?

Examine these odd shapes. Then see if you can see a word spelled out. What is the word?

Answers

Working It Out

5. Nine Cards in A Square
The nine cards should be placed in the order shown below.

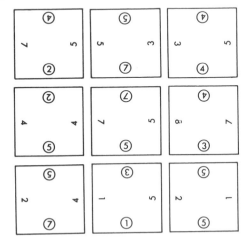

6. Rectangles
There are 36 rectangles altogether.

7. The Hexagon
There are 38 triangles in the hexagon.

8. The Bookworm
As we look at the books as they stand on the shelf, the first page of volume 1 is on the right of that volume, so the bookworm travels only through the front cover of volume 1. It now travels through the back cover of volume 2, all through the pages of volume 2, through the front cover of volume 2, and lastly through the back cover of volume 3. So the distance totals:

Front cover, volume 1	2 mm
Back cover, volume 2	2 mm
Pages, volume 2	302 mm
Front cover, volume 2	2 mm
Back cover, volume 1	2 mm
Total	310 mm

11. Dividing It Up
There were only three people involved in sharing the money. They were a son, a father and a grandfather. Each is a son (of someone), while the other two are fathers as well.

13. Strange Symbols
The symbols are simply the numbers 1, 2, 3, 4, and 5 drawn face to face with their mirror images. So the final symbol should be **ᘓ6** which is the figure 6 plus its reverse image.

14. The Difference
A difference of 20. Twice twenty-five is fifty, and twice five, and twenty, makes thirty.

15. Dozens
$$\text{Six dozen dozen} = 6 \times 12 \times 12 = 864$$
$$\text{Half a dozen dozen} = 6 \times 12 = 72$$
$$864 - 72 = 792$$

16. Herrings
The last person of the five received his herring on the original dish.

17. Making Six into Three
You simply take the six strokes and form the word THREE from them:

THREE

18. A Strange Sum
The Roman numerals XIX signify 19. If you take away the I it leaves XX, which is twenty.

19. Cutting The Cloth
59 seconds. The last cut separates the last two metre lengths, so a 60th cut is not required.

20. Strange Addition
You add the Roman V to I, making IV, which is four. IX in Roman numerals is 9, but adding the letter S makes SIX.

21. The Mouse
There were nine ears of corn in the box. Although the mouse brought three ears on each journey, two of them were her own.

22. More Strange Symbols

The symbols actually spell GLASS. Only the lower half of the letters have been used, and the upper half shows its mirror image. Here is the word spelled in ordinary letters, but with a line drawn through the centre. Place a pocket mirror along the line, and, seen together, you will find a line of symbols.

23. The Eight Matches

Here are the eight matches. If you space them out like this, you will have:

two   &   *a half-dozen*

24. Circle of Coins

This will not work unless a special system of counting is used. Almost always the counting will end on a coin already turned over. To solve the puzzle, you count in the order shown in the diagram. Count 1, 2, 3 and 4, and turn over the fourth coin. Now MISS THREE COINS, starting again at No. 8. No. 1 will then be turned over. Miss three coins, and start again at No. 5, so that No. 8 is then turned over. The sequence then is as follows:

Start again at No. 2, and turn over No. 5
Start again at No. 9, and turn over No. 2
Start again at No. 6, and turn over No. 9
Start again at No. 3, and turn over No. 6
Start again at No. 10, and turn over No. 3
Start again at No. 7, and turn over No. 10

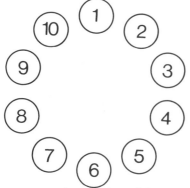

You have now turned over nine of the ten coins. This puzzle works better if you make up a set of small counters, numbered, and with, say, red on one side and blue on the other.

25. The Squares and Triangles

The diagram contains 36 squares and 92 triangles.

26. Family Party

The party included three children (two girls and a boy), their father and mother, and their father's father and mother. Each of these people can be seen to have the relationship shown:

1 grandfather, who was also a father and a father-in-law;
1 grandmother, who was also a mother and a mother-in-law;
1 father, who was also a son and a child;
1 mother, who was also a daughter-in-law;
1 son, who was also a brother and a child;
2 daughters who were also sisters and children.

27. The Portrait

The picture showed the owner's son. What he has really said is 'The father of that man is my father's son.' In this case, the father of the subject must be either a brother of the owner, or himself. But he has already told us that he has no brother, so he must be the father himself.

28. Hard-Boiled Eggs

Only one. After eating that, the person's stomach is no longer empty.

29. Three Houses and the Pipes

There are several ways that the pipes can be taken to the houses, and the illustration (below left) shows one.

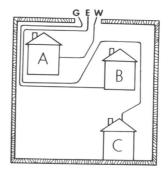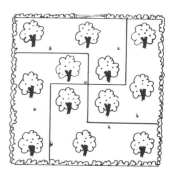

30. Forwarding the Mail

No, it was not. Arthur should have realised that, having sent his key to the office by post, it would arrive in the locked mailbox, and Jenny would be quite unable to get it out.

31. The Orchard

The diagram (above right) now shows how the division was made.

32. Balancing a Stewpot
The four pieces of iron are interlaced as shown in the diagram, when they will reach the four posts, and also support each other and the stewpot.

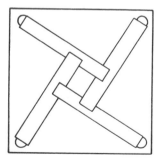

33. The Farmhouse
The land was divided as shown in the diagram.

34. The Two Belgians
The two Belgians were husband and wife.

35. The Pigs in the Sties
He still hadn't placed the tenth pig anywhere.

36. The Phone-In
If the man had a widow, he would be in no position to marry again. He'd be dead!

37. The Home Secretary
If the murders were undetected, there could be no figures available, since no one knew they had been committed.

38. The Ship's Ladder
Since the ladder rose with the ship, the same number of rungs would remain submerged however many hours passed.

39. Balancing the Books
There is no reason at all why the 'amount left' column should balance with the first. Mrs Tompkins had £10 and spent £10. There was nothing left.

40. The Dream
If the man in the story had really died in his sleep, how did anyone else know what his dream had been about?

41. At the Bank
Miss Robinson, of course, proved nothing, except that the photograph was of her.

42. The Roman Coin
The coin was an obvious fake. '48 BC' means '48 years before the birth of Christ.' No one knew when Christ was coming, so there was no way the coins could be dated in that way. In any case, the letters 'BC' form the initial letters of the English words 'Before Christ.' English did not even exist in 48 BC.

43. The Two Indians
Strong East Wind was Happy Hunter's mother.

44. The Factory
He was stealing wheelbarrows.

Tricks and Games

45. The Clasped Hands
Clasp the hands around the leg of a heavy table or similar object.

46. Problem With Hands
His/her right elbow.

47. Fives
The cards should be placed together as shown in the diagram, where one pip on each card is covered.

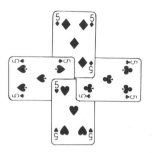

48. Aces and Courts
Take the four Aces, and make a diagonal row, starting from the top left hand corner. The order of suits doesn't matter, but let us suppose that we have chosen the order Ace of Spades, Ace of Clubs, Ace of Hearts and Ace of Diamonds. Next, we take the Kings, and form another diagonal row, but running in the opposite direction from the first. The two red Kings must be opposite the

Ace of Spades	Jack of Hearts	Queen of Diamonds	King of Clubs
Jack of Diamonds	Ace of Clubs	King of Spades	Queen of Hearts
Queen of Clubs	King of Diamonds	Ace of Hearts	Jack of Spades
King of Hearts	Queen of Spades	Jack of Clubs	Ace of Diamonds

red Aces, and the black Kings opposite the black Aces. So our diagonal row of Kings, starting from the top right hand corner will run: King of Clubs, King of Spades, King of Diamonds and King of Hearts. Now place the four Queens, starting with the two positions next to the top right hand corner. The Queen of Diamonds is placed immediately to the left of the King of Clubs, and the Queen of Hearts is placed immediately below that King. We then do similarly with the bottom left hand corner. Place the Queen of Clubs immediately above the King of Hearts, and the Queen of Spades immediately to the right of that King. We are now left only with the Jacks. It should not take long to work out where they are to be placed. The Jack of Hearts is placed between the Ace of Spades and the Queen of Diamonds in the top row. The Jack of Diamonds is placed at the beginning of row 2; the Jack of Spades at the end of row 3, and the Jack of Clubs between the Queen of Spades and the Ace of Diamonds in the bottom row. The pattern will vary, according to the original positioning of the Aces.

49. Paper Shapes

The four shapes should be placed together as shown here.

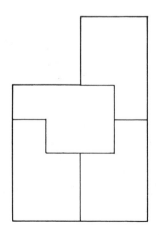

50. Floating Corks

It seems impossible at first, but all you need to do is to take all seven corks together in both hands, in an upright bundle. Hold them under water in the basin for a minute or two to make them quite wet, and then bring them back to the surface very slowly. If you do this carefully, you will find that the whole bundle will stay together, and float upright.

51. Man of Many Parts

The various pictures should be interlaced as shown in the illustration below.

53. Cork and Bottle

Blowing upon the cork will almost certainly force the cork *out* of the bottle, instead of into it. In fact, the stronger the blowing, the quicker will the cork come out. This is because the act of blowing forces some air into the bottle, making the air inside more compressed. The more you blow, the more air is forced in, and so the cork is pushed *out*. But the trick can be done. Take a drinking straw and blow steadily through this against the *centre* of the cork. This time, the cork will go in without trouble.

54. Knotting the Ring

The person with the cord should hold it about three inches from the upper end and the one with the ring passes the ring over it, and then takes hold of the upper end of the cord, drawing it through the first person's fingers to within an inch or two of the opposite end. The cord should be held slack, with the ring hanging in the centre of the loop. The second person then passes the end he or she holds around the opposite part of the loop and draws it through. The knot is now tied.

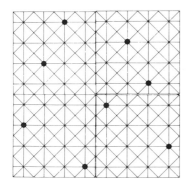

55. The Treasure Map

The correct arrangement of the parts of the map is as shown in the diagram above.

56. Balancing a Pencil

Open the penknife, and stick the point of the blade into the pencil about a third of the way up from the point, as shown in the illustration. The penknife should be partially closed. The exact amount that the penknife should be opened or closed can be judged by experimenting, so that the pencil point, when placed upon the finger-tip, will balance.

58. Lifting the Coin

If you interlace the straws as shown in the illustration, the five pence coin forms a kind of wedge, which locks the straws and coins together. You can then take one straw and lift the four plus the coin.

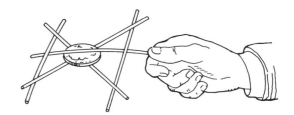

59. Two Dogs

The dotted lines show where the extra four lines will appear. The dogs now appear to be alive and running at speed.

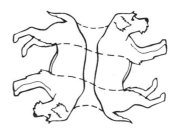

60. Unspillable Water

Fill a glass with water, right up to the brim. Lay a piece of strong card flat upon the top. Place your hand on the top of the card, and holding it in place, turn the glass

57. Cutting a Postcard

The card is cut carefully with a sharp knife, as shown. Fold the card down the centre, and cut through the folded line to within 5 mm of each end. It will look like the card marked 'A' in the illustration. Next, with the card folded, make further cuts all along the card 3 mm apart as shown in the diagram marked 'B'. The cuts should be made alternately from the edge of the card and the centre, each cut stopping within 5 mm of the opposite edge. When all the cuts have been made, open out the card, and it will look like the diagram C. If you open it out still farther, very carefully, you will be able to form a large loop, large enough for the average person to pass through.

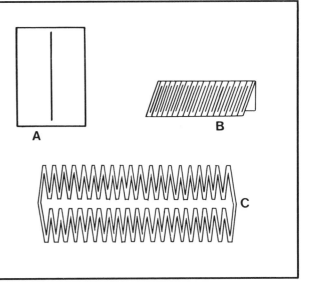

over. You can now remove your hand, and the water will not run out, nor will the card fall away. Now put the inverted glass near the edge of a smooth working surface, preferably by the kitchen sink. Carefully draw away the card, and the water should remain in position without running out. Of course, the glass cannot now be lifted without all the water running out.

61. Holding a Coin
Take the two diagonally opposite corners of the handkerchief between each finger and thumb (keeping the thumb on the upper surface in each case), and stretch the handkerchief strongly. The centre of the handkerchief will form into several strong folds or pleats. The coin will remain in position as you lift the handkerchief, and even if you turn it sideways, the coin will not fall out.

62. Looping the Scissors
Pass the loop through the opposite bow of the scissors, and over the ends of the scissors, and the cord will come free.

63. The Hole in the Paper
Fold the paper exactly across the centre of the hole. Take the paper in both hands, and ask someone to drop the 10p coin into the fold. Let the coin rest just over the hole, so that its lower edge projects below. Bend the corners of the paper slightly upwards. Soon, the 10p coin will drop through, because bending the paper upwards has made the hole a little longer.

Visual Ilusions

70. Top Hat
Both are of equal length.

71. The Three Squares
They are are all true squares, but the horizontal and vertical lines make them appear to have different dimensions.

72. The Lampshade
They are both of equal length.

76. The Cubes
The number of cubes depends upon how you see the illustration.

77. The Booklet
The booklet can be seen both ways.

78. Rings in the Tube
Again, the eyes will see the tube either way. The illusion can change if you blink your eyes.

79. The Staircase
This is an illusion similar to those shown above. The staircase can appear either way.

81. Which Line Continues?
(a) Yes – the sloping lines would meet. (b) If you place a ruler through the lines, you can see which lines continues. In (c) it is the lower left-hand line which continues.

92. Where Is the Middle Rod?
The rod does not join the base at all. It is a kind of false or trick perspective, and really a totally impossible figure.

91. The Triangle
This again is a totally impossible figure, and could not really exist as a three-dimensional form.

93. Odd Shapes Or Word
What is shown is the word LEFT spelled out in block letters. If a black line is added at the top and bottom, the word can be seen quite clearly.